THE LIKELY FUTURE

THE LIKELY FUTURE

Short and Long Term Guidance from the Source

PENELOPE JEAN HAYES

WITH CAROLE SERENE AS CHANNELER

—volume 1—

Cover design by:
Andrew Green
www.AndrewGreenArt.co.uk

Printed in the United States of America

First Printing, 2020

ISBN-13: 978-1-949001-16-7 print edition
ISBN-13: 978-1-949001-17-4 ebook edition
ISBN-13: 978-1-949001-18-1 audio edition

 Waterside Publishing

Waterside Productions
2055 Oxford Ave
Cardiff, CA 92007
www.waterside.com

For Humanity—
So that you know you are not alone.

CONTENTS

FOREWORD FROM PUBLISHER

This is one of the most important books you will ever read.

As the literary agent for Eckhart Tolle, Neale Donald Walsch, and many other visionary teachers and best selling authors, I have been privileged to review, agent and publish books like *A NEW EARTH*, *CONVERSATIONS WITH GOD*, and *THE LIFE CHANGING MAGIC OF TIDYING UP*. With all of these best sellers there have been transmissions of pure wisdom from a higher source. Whether these transmissions were unique to the individual authors or represent these authors tapping into "universal mind" or the zero point, can be debated. In my opinion, all great writing comes from a higher source. Sometimes that higher source is clearly outside of the personality domain of the actual author. In those cases, the information is often considered channeled. I am not asking readers and listeners to believe that channelers exist; I was skeptical of channeled information for many years and still am. However, there are ways to discern truth from speculation.

In reviewing materials of PAX—submitted by author Penelope Jean Hayes and channeler Carole Serene—in collaboration with my wife and Waterside's publisher, Gayle Gladstone, we have determined that PAX is a pure source of information. PAX is motivated by love and compassion for the Earth and all living creatures.

When COVID-19 became a pandemic we asked for guidance. The book, or audio that you are listening to, contains that guidance. PAX provided this information prior to any public statements by Harvard University scientists, or others, as to the complex nature of the virus and why the recovery will take much longer than any of us would have liked.

For many, the information in this book, and future PAX books, will be controversial. We encourage the pursuit of truth and believe that all of us should test all information for logic and factual accuracy, especially when dealing with life and death issues such as those relevant to the spread and hopefully eventual end to the current pandemic.

This is a must-read book and contains not just warnings that will keep you safe, but reasons to hope.

On the highest level, your individual thoughts and actions will always have important influence on your life outcome. Maintaining your highest level of awareness and continuing to focus on your ability to help yourself and others with positive life affirming thoughts will always have value. Now, more than ever, is the time to express gratitude for all the beauty and grace that flows from the miracle of nature and of life.

—William and Gayle Gladstone, Publishers,
Waterside Productions, Inc.

INTRODUCTION

THE LIKELY FUTURE is an urgent message from the "Source." You might call this Spirit presence "The Almighty," "God," "Yahweh," or another name for the Divine—in our writings, we say Pax.

The dialogue that is this concise book came through while we were writing *Do Unto Earth*, a series of manuscripts of channeled wisdom about planetary wellness and repair, plus many curiosities of our human history.

You could say that when in early 2020 the coronavirus/COVID-19 pandemic had begun to spread widely around the globe, Pax interrupted our usual writings for a special broadcast.

Before we jump right into this important and extraordinary conversation—a process where I ask the questions and Carole Serene channels Spirit by way of automatic writing—it's appropriate that you know who's speaking. The best way to explain the source of these wisdoms is to let you hear it directly from the Source. By way of introduction, the following is an excerpt from *Do Unto Earth: It's Not Too Late*.

(Note to reader: Penelope is bold print. Pax is indented.)

It would seem that many people do not live in harmony with nature and with respect and love for the Earth. Why do we matter to God when we are so destructive to ourselves, others, and our planetary home?

> Well now, this is indeed an interesting question for it is well known that your God considers everything worth mattering. Penelope, it is the overall love that defines Planet Earth's people as those to whom God matters, so it is their understanding they also matter to God. We suggest each organized religion has their own name for who they follow, and this question relates to the love each deity has for followers. Love is unconditional; this is why you matter.

I suspect that there's a reason why you've said "*your* God," and certainly, this piques my interest. I am aware that I'm speaking to a great Spirit Messenger and Spirit Energy from the Spirit World; however, I'd like to know more about you.

> **Were you once from Earth, from a former and far more evolved people? Please help me to understand the source of your wisdom so that Earth's people will listen.**

> We do not incarnate as solid and we do not "reside" in one place—this is our gift. "My"

origins do not include your planet, no, but having watched the development of society and where you are today, it is clear that a guiding hand is needed.

It is the case that my/our interest in communicating with Earth's people today is to share wisdom. Is this not the way to growth and evolution, to share with others what one has learned? Our speak, our words, our wisdoms are generated for the purpose of sharing guidance and the path to wellness for your planet. We have no linear time and refer only to soon time and far time. We in the Spirit World have duty and obligation to assist those in need and where requested, to offer wisdom to assist others. I care as we should all care, as should Earth's people care about your future.

Okay, so you were never a physical being or from Planet Earth, you are and have always been Spirit. Would it be accurate to think of you as the Guardian Angel for Earth?

Ah, no, that is not our role. *Conscience* in each of you, when activated, is collectively a guardian angel for Mother Earth.

There needs to be continued action and awareness to this end. Without being aware, your people have placed your planet in jeopardy and are moving forward with life as usual. There are some who wrap their lives around the correction of damage done and the prevention of future evils in this regard. They are the saints and saviors of your world but are not enough by themselves.

Consciousness needs raising in a maximum way to allow your people to have the meeting of minds which will create the global power necessary to effect change. Together you are a force. Come together in your thinking—the rest will follow.

Has a cosmic course been plotted for this message at this time and why did you choose me?

We knew, we waited, and when the time was right to write (cosmic smile here), we met and it is good.

Penelope, in many past lifetimes, you have been a champion of causes, and a common thread running through them was your love and concern for the wild animals of the Earth. Your transferring of that to and inclusion of domestic animals, has you on a long-established course of action for yourself. You have lived as an aboriginal and First Nations person. You have seen the ways wounded by those who would move in and take over the land, destroying all that came before. You have experienced the hostility and shame of being hunted and removed from your known life in place and time. You can feel these feelings and know that the vibration of Mother Earth now reflects these feelings. You have watched Earth being done unto in a very bad way in past lifetimes, and you bring with you the depth of feeling to expose what is, today.

Your greatest gift is the ability to raise the consciousness of a population and bring the message of healing to your world. You have the purity, the energy, the ability and the resources. We think that is a good basis for trust in action for now and into our future works together.

Penelope, you have many questions, there will be no end to these questions, and they are all dedicated to the cause you feel and work you wish to continue on behalf of your planet.

Is this a heavy load? Not for Penelope who, after considering all of this information for a time, will understand and accept your challenge. You are the one. We support your journey and are pleased to be a part, with Carole Serene. Trust in this and go in peace and love.

Gosh, that *is* a commission. (And, I do have a lot of questions.)

You have a confidence and directness that is very compelling. I'll go ahead and ask outright: who are you, exactly?

We are one with the Universe, not the Universe alone. We are the Divine Universe, yes, and the

God being and the greater wisdom, that which knows and supports all and is healing, non-judgmental and tolerant, all-seeing, all-knowing, and Peace.

(Gulp!)

Who-You-Are makes our discussion extraordinary: "*We are the Divine Universe, not the Universe alone, the God being and the greater wisdom.*" I'm humbled and honored to be having this dialogue with you.

So then, you *are* whom we would call God?

This question does not regard that there are other religions and groups who do not define themselves as related to "God." You are to know that organized religion on your Earth plane relates to other deities and those who study the Bible, Quran and many other holy texts, and consider themselves related to their own varieties of your God. Think of Shiva or Allah and remember—variations on the theme are reality.

We are wisdom and history and benevolence. We are not a deity. We are who we report to be and have always reported to be. We are forever, we are infinity and we are always and will be always—this is infinity and this is us.

Oh, I see, "God being" and "God" have different connotations, and "Divine" and "deity" are not synonymous. This is a revelation.

Perception, it is, that defines us in the hearts and minds of your people. Our Universe is not of the proportion of what you might expect and *our range also greater in both future and past and all-being.*

We wish to engage in action as opposed to brackets and confines of description. To define further is folly as it is the finite amount of fear your people have around deities and religions as organized and what may and may not be permitted within those confines. It is our functioning outside of these discussions that is preferred. Your earthly religions hold value and offer solace to the many. For those who function outside of those realms, our energy is defined and available.

We support and offer love, unconditional love for this is how our Universe functions.

I'm understanding that the issue of a name is about ensuring inclusivity to all people and inclusion of those following any one of the many world religions and the name that each calls their deity or Divine Being, and those who follow no religion at all. Today, these names cause division. Am I getting your point correctly?

We are here to say the rose smells as sweet without our name of Rose.

That's a simple yet effective analogy. Still, I'd like to know how I should address you. May you provide an

approved moniker for the purpose of these volumes, one that crosses borders and religions and can connect all to the message?

Pax.

Pax reflects our goodwill and wish for peace. Yes, this is us—Pax. Relate to this as Spirit Messenger of Truth, Peace and Goodwill. It is our mission, and yours.

We are blessed to be with you and it has become your mission to ensure our words reach those in need, our direction is heard, and a potential global disaster averted if people can be activated and energized and empowered to begin to have their voices heard and the movement toward planetary repair enlarged.

PART ONE
THE BEGINNING

Dear Pax, together we have been writing a series of manuscripts, which as you have indicated are of the utmost gravity for the people of Earth. As we do so, there are times when your message for humanity is of an even timelier manner and can't wait for the upcoming publication of our books.

What message do you have for humanity today?

There are movements above and below your world that demand attention. They begin with the global pandemic taking lives and hearts around your Planet Earth. Your world has now seen a culling of population through an illness, a virus, and looking back in your history it has been the way.

For now your people are to understand the big picture and practice what they are instructed to do by those who understand good health and wellness. It is the time to be contrite and realize the damage to your planet is beginning to remediate—this is not the time to consider it over and normal is normal again. Your normal of recent times is gone. No such normal will exist when quarantines are lifted. There is a new normal, which you will see includes change in all aspects of life. Yes, there will be resumption of old ways in *some* respects and there will be resumption of closer human bonds. Reality is that life will go on.

Of course, you're speaking of coronavirus/COVID-19.

It is only the harshest of preventions now and lock-downs and quarantines that will stop this. As it is now, some areas are clearing but it is to be known that what comes from below is another, a deeper virus that follows as a resurgence of what is now being fought. Lingering in the cells of those infected are anenomies that will open and grow and re-infect when it is thought clarity of disease and good health have returned.

I'm not familiar with this term. What are anenomies?

These residual anenomies are the lingering buds of virus that remain closed and quiet until such time as they are triggered to burst open and begin the process of infection all over again.

What would trigger these anenomies to open and re-infect?

Time only, these buds are latent and like trees in the Spring season open their buds to the world, it is a time-related incubation coming to end and that end is a bloom. That bloom is then a beginning, a resurgence of infection.

Does this cycle repeat more than once in an infected person?

It can and will if not completely eradicated, both rampant infection and cocooned and latent virus.

Is there a treatment effective in eliminating all aspects of the COVID-19, including the latent buds?

At this time it is not understood by your science that this underlying virus condition exists. You are too new in this exploration of cause and effect and cure to have found the bigger picture and how to ameliorate the danger. There will be progress made in laboratories developing vaccines, but this is not the whole picture. It is the case that prevention is worth much now and care must be taken to isolate and quarantine and remove from circulation those who have been exposed.

In the bigger picture there becomes a reality of not knowing all. This is the impediment to the development of a fix—not enough time has passed to relate what is now to what is hidden and will become the next wave of infection. Let it be known there will be a next wave and the appropriate precautions must be taken.

We wish to state also that the worst is to come in the mismanagement of this global curse to wellness. There are world leaders considering the wrong way of managing this specifically to create their own crowns and be anointed from the fountain of greatness. This is to play out and the sadness in your world is that it will do so. Meanwhile, there is time to be devoted to funding research and development of the understanding of the depths of this virus and its intensity.

There is a darkness to this disease that requires careful handling, now in your Earth time. Immediate care is to be taken in continuing the medical work and science required to see the bigger picture within this virus and how it attacks, hides then attacks again. It must be the focus of your world at this time.

Is there not anything that we can do now to protect those that have had COVID-19 so that they would not catch it again?

The fact is not that this virus is "caught again," but that it has not left the body and re-infects, as a bud opens in Spring, triggered by time passing and indicating the next phase has arrived.

That stretch of time can be interrupted by science—it has the ability to insert a pathogen that scrambles the signal to open and infect, thereby rendering it harmless. And this will become the final end of the virus in the body, not simply a delay of reappearing.

What more can you tell our scientists about the ability to insert a pathogen that scrambles the signal?

As your science begins to understand this virus, and the knowledge of a second phase is realized, the support of laboratories begins to isolate and mimic the behavior and see the way to interruption of the cycle. It's not rocket science for them but rather the first understanding of the way to ensure it is not in the repeating department.

The recognition of the ability of this virus to become mute and then blossom again, funding of the research and development of interruption, and dedication of researchers to this cause is key. Without this there is not a finality to hosting this disease. It will be done and the research involved will find its way to other disease where it can interrupt the flow and bring cure. There are neurological diseases that benefit from the introduction of this solution found for the virus. Always there is an upside.

Oh, really? Which neurological diseases can benefit from this solution?

We state that the neurological interrupters targeted by a vaccine will be written, if you wish. It is the Parkinson's type of disease entity that would be affected. There is a neurotransmitter that experiences short-circuiting and interruption. This can be found to respond. It is a sideways and unexpected effect, we say it is, and sometimes this is the medical miracle found in research. There is more to this as there is always more. Time brings further seeking and seekers and light is shined into the question.

In our *Do Unto Earth* series you speak at length about diseases, including another recommended treatment (and an environmentally-based eradication) for Parkinson's disease, to name one illness. I'm sure our readers will be enlightened to know that more regarding our health and wellness will be shared in other writings.

Pax, I'm going to take a deep breath here and then I must ask you something rather important.

Here goes—

We don't really know for sure what caused the global coronavirus outbreak. We have not found the definitive "patient zero." A leading theory is that the virus began through an animal-to-human interface via the "wet markets" in China, specifically those in Wuhan, Hubei province. Many people around the world had not heard of wet markets prior, yet now we've been apprised of these open markets where live animals are sold for food. These animals might include live fish, bats, snakes, monkeys, cats, dogs, koala, and other wildlife, some that are endangered species. Another theory of what led to this outbreak is that coronavirus was being studied on bats (or another animal?) in a research facility laboratory close by to a wet market, and that a researcher was accidentally contaminated with the virus and therefore it got out to the community and then the world.

May you please clear up for us precisely how the coronavirus/COVID-19 outbreak began?

> In this case it was to be a weapon of war—the management of the laboratory process went wrong. This will never be acknowledged as truth. It was intended as a macro-method of creating a defenseless opponent.
>
> The far-reaching implications of this began to be realized in that control of it was not as manageable as had been believed. It became clear that this would become problematic and steps were taken to diminish the virus, to kill it and these were not successful. It escaped the Petri dish into the masses of humanity and the rest is history.

The laboratory that you refer to is in China?

> Yes. This is known by your government officials. Your USA officials, that is.

To be clear—even though you're telling us that the Chinese government created this virus as a "weapon of war," with the intention of creating a "defenseless opponent"—they did not intend to use this weapon at this time? This abomination got out of the lab and it was a non-intentional *mistake* when it did?

> Indeed this is so, and the proximity to wet markets and disposal of laboratory subject animals was the next major contributor to this beginning.
>
> There is the question of this being a natural virus—one found in nature, that is—being studied in this lab for its ability to *transform* into something beyond its origins. For it to be used as an infector of humanity was being investigated; the power of it was unknown. To take it out of nature and combine it with catalysts such as was done, involved an impact not considered.

Whoa, let's back up a step. Please confirm that you are saying that this lab dumped virus-contaminated live lab animals in the wet markets. This is unimaginable. What kind of animals? Did they not know that

these animals would infect people? So, wait—then it
***was* intentional?**

> The *deed* was done intentionally; if it was truly
> known that the infection *was in place* in those
> bats, remains to be seen.

But, *why* did they dump lab animals into local area wet
markets? To dispose of evidence? To not waste what
could be used for food because perhaps they didn't
know the animals were in fact infected? Out of a sort
of laziness for a resolution about what to do with the
no longer needed animals?

> The why of it is less important than the where
> and when. That a lab worker made a decision
> to do this, without knowledge of others, is the
> situation. Was there knowledge of the infection
> being what it was? Not likely. An error had been
> made and a way to cover it was sought. Human
> error is often at the basis of tragedy. In this case
> the error was to cover a change in lab protocol—
> this was the genesis of the virus and what was
> trying to be covered by removal of the subjects.
>
> At this time the energy is to be devoted to
> cure and less to human involvement in cause.
> One step at a time.
>
> It is not wise to be analyzing so much now
> as it is to be finding that which will oppose the
> virus. Would there be cooperation between the

laboratory and a world health organization that could learn the truth with the understanding it was an accident? Possibly, if pursued.

To shortcut in this manner would be advisable if it could be orchestrated.

All right, I'll leave it there in hopes for cooperation and full disclosure. As abominable as it is, I suppose that the developing of biological weapons goes on in many countries, albeit this kind of a mistake is unprecedented. Honesty and openness, even now, will go a long way in forgiveness and healing.

Going forward, how can we avoid this situation and protect ourselves, protect the world population?

Political defenses are the way. There must be agreements that such virus testing for warring purposes will not take place. Human error plays an important role and human nature is too undisciplined to be in a position of control of such a weapon.

It is staggering how people all over the world became infected with COVID-19, even indigenous peoples living in villages deep inside the Amazon rainforest.

An airborne virus that mutates is no match for those with no knowledge of prevention.

Is there a connection between animal hosts and the severity of COVID-19?

There is a connection, yes. The outbreak began with animal hosts and in your present development it is seen that a large cluster of the virus in the USA is in a pork processing plant.

This common denominator is the flesh and blood, the ability of the virus to grab onto the cells and become mutated. This ability to manifest itself as a lethal weapon is exacerbated by the host body. It is a feature of the virus that it will become more toxic and lethal in a setting such as this.

May you please explain how it works with household companion animals and if this is a worry factor?

As we have defined, it is the setting of such a crowded and dense animal processing plant that allows for cross-contamination in a rapid manner.

Household pets are no more at risk for contracting or transmitting virus than household people. It is wise, however, to not subject pets, as people, to others from outside of the home. Touching is to be avoided except within the family unit.

PART TWO
THE SCIENCE

Pax, there is a curiosity currently showing itself in some hospitals: young, healthy pregnant women arriving for obstetric care and birthing, although asymptomatic, tested positive for the virus in large numbers. Is there a correlation between their production of a new life and the virus attaching to them?

Indeed there is, and while they were asymptomatic, in some instances their babies were not. This is a study going forward that will have implications for future testing.

Is the current virus testing effective for the goal of isolating those with the virus?

It is not, and further—it is looking in the wrong direction.

This virus has more than one phase, and it is the initial phase and level of antibodies being considered. When a recovered individual is considered virus free it remains as a lurking danger to that person as it will bloom again. There is no other way to view this—it is to be considered that all is not done when the remission comes, for it is not a cure, merely remission.

It is now thought that this virus is most contagious when a person is pre-symptomatic. Is this true, and is there immunity—at last—after the *second* outbreak?

The infected person, while asymptomatic, is highly contagious and this is the danger. There must be a test showing contamination has taken place so early confinement may begin. Isolation is the key.

Antibody tests will show immunity at stages of this development but there is not to be a sense of "all is well." There are mutations of this virus, which might not stop at two stages within a patient.

Is a COVID-19 positive person, after recovery, and while then asymptomatic for a time, still contagious *between* outbreaks?

It is the hiding of the truth of what is to come, yes. It is a false sense of security, if you will. During this time the virus is dormant, the person is still contagious, and appears asymptomatic—dangerous to all involved.

It must be understood by your science that there is a second outbreak coming. The dormancy of the virus—the sneak attack—is to be understood and acted upon.

Some unique symptoms, such as loss of smell and taste, are early warning signs for some who have contracted the virus, but not others. How is this to be understood?

We say the differing strains of this virus have not yet been discussed.

It comes in varieties, which makes the understanding of it complicated. What the sensory loss indicates is a lesser volatile strain, one that will not attack as fiercely and will avoid the lungs. It does, however, want to visit mucous membranes in the upper respiratory system and rhino-nasal areas. This is to be watched.

All of the medical testing that needs to be done in order to make headway with COVID-19 will be done on lab animals, likely monkeys. It's another layer of heartbreak to this crisis, I think. Is this the way of these scientific tests or is there another way?

Well, it is normally the case, or has been in your past, that this is the way of it. There is less of an appetite in present times for this method, however, and change is made. What is current is less of the old type of testing and more of a developmental model including the use of a lab animal as the last step when it is believed the successful formula is found.

When we have global health crises, we often run low on blood donations. Can blood be reverse engineered and manufactured? What is it that we don't understand that might make this a possible solution?

Well, it is the case that blood can be created, yes, and your science is focusing on such an eventuality, although, at present, in your Earth time, it has not come to the top of the list of projects under consideration.

To take what is, in terms of blood types, and attempt to recreate is doable but the human body is not prepared for synthetics. Until such time as this sensitivity is overcome, and that is another study entirely, there will be no ability to introduce a substitute for human blood into a human body.

Much like the ability for humans to be made immune to virus, the time involved in study and development is immense, many generations will pass, and it is slow progress. Which is most important of the two—chicken or egg conundrum—all things are to be considered in repairing the rent in the fabric of human health.

You know, the medical communities are asking for blood donations from people who have recovered from COVID-19, convalescent blood that they say will be a treatment given to others to prevent contracting the virus by way of creating an immunity/antibody. However, because the virus can stay dormant and re-blooms in time, is blood donation from those whom have been infected advisable?

Is this "convalescent" blood? This meaning is that the donor has recovered.

This is dangerous now, as the truth is not yet understood regarding the lingering of this virus within a body. While there is a quiet time between blooms there may also be a third and this must be considered. At this time, the administering of plasma from one to another is to be regarded as questionable.

More is to be known about the virus origin and its ability to disguise itself within the host body.

PART THREE
THE FUTURE

Pax, there are countries in lock-down and countries coming back from the worst. There are areas of countries trusting that isolation from one another is the way of prevention, and other areas denouncing this as foolish. How can there be freedom from fear of infection and reinfection when there is no continuity in prevention?

Human nature is such that challenge will remain—challenge to finding wellness and challenge to maintaining a lifestyle of purpose and fulfillment. There is far to go in this deliberation of what is right and who believes it is so. Much common sense is lacking in your leaders and there is far to go in this resolution also.

At this time we say much time will pass with many lives lost, while some world leaders place their own wellbeing above that of their people.

There is justice to come and it is in the form of the virus itself. A great equalizer, it is.

A jaw-dropping statement. And, I'm going to leave that alone, also.

As we look to the months (and years) ahead, how can inequality be overcome to the extent there is continuity of preventive practices?

We suggest your Earth people have the voices to be heard. We say that change comes at the top while those who go about their daily lives have the ability to care for themselves. It is the case that many do not, and this is where empathy between neighbors must again rise. Voices of reason will rise from the people where not previously heard. This is where the mission becomes reality and those who should be heard, will be. The expression was, "power to the people," and this speaks to each individual's ability to make a difference in their world, their community, and be the voice of reason. This is your time.

Reopening of business and entertainment and life as it was is not to be undertaken lightly in an effort to bolster economy. Human life is of utmost importance and there is need to believe in this and act upon it.

Alternate ways of living and working and playing are now becoming obvious. Some will be discarded at a later date while others form the basis of your new normal.

In time, it will be a better normal, you will see.

If isolation is our best defense against this virus pandemic, what about people's incomes? Many people are in jobs where they might not be able to work from home. Should everyone find a way to pivot in terms of the job that they do for a living? Should every job, or most, evolve to meet this changed way of life?

As is currently becoming the way of life in your world, change is being made in all areas including the workplace. Your people are resilient and create alternate means of doing business and ways harnessed now to provide continued income for business and workers. The use of social media contributes to awareness of how small business, particularly, is adapting. Working remotely, from home, is a twist that will be retained when your world again opens to commerce. There are no reasons at this time for people to go around the rules of distancing or isolation in order to work; this would be counterproductive and is not condoned by employers or health experts. Time shows the way. It is now being celebrated how creativity takes the place of routine, and new ways of doing old tasks, prevail.

I wonder, what is the lasting impact on both Earth and her current population as a result of the coronavirus pandemic?

In time it will be shown that there are positive impacts of the lifestyle changes demanded by the response to this virus outbreak. Activity reduction brings cleaner air and less pollution of all kinds. The soil and water rejuvenate and a rebirth takes place. There is a clearing and cleaning of the atmosphere and this continues. It becomes a catalyst for the new breed of awareness among people and their way of living. It brings good energy, which is a bonus now on your planet.

We have lost and continue to loose many people to this global pandemic, and still, we hope to find a larger meaning. What's the proverbial silver lining regarding the world population's infliction with coronavirus?

At this time in your world history there came an awareness, one that is based on people relying on people, that no one person is alone and without hope.

That those in the lowest level of society became as or more valued than those in the stratosphere based upon the job they do and human services they provide. This time and way of adapting shows that the great equalization has begun: a new awareness of status and value of people based on their contributions to humanity. The equalizer is the services provided with humanitarian care and concern by those previously deemed to be less than. This is not the way to think of other humans; all are created equal. Time shows who rises, like cream to the top, and who does not offer themselves to the cause. Clarity is the outcome.

Your world continues to turn and as the clarity of what has come and gone and changed your society settles in, there are aha moments among your people, moments that show how the mighty can fall while the lowest on the economic ladder rise to fulfill a duty they claimed as their own and made a positive difference in the lives of many. These situations show people's true colors. Your world is now shaped by a level of goodness that has resurged and will continue to be the barometer by which people function. What begins as a mistake (or was it?) shapes the future of your planet and shows that equality is the true measure of a civilization.

Is living together in complete equality the shared purpose for humans on Earth?

The world population is intended to function as a family with patience and love for all. This is not what it has grown into over the last century in your Earth time. Now that a culling has taken place and a reversal of roles in many areas, those in lower echelons of society are being viewed as heroes and those in the upper reaches of the wealthy are being recognized as not so useful overall, a shift in attitude is upon you. How value is placed on individuals and professions has changed. How those who did not highly value *themselves* as a result of societal treatment, are now responding to the love being expressed and shown to them from people recognizing their selflessness and worth.

It takes a tragedy, often, for your people to recognize the truth around them and leave behind their superficial attitudes and behaviors. This should not be.

Empowering those who give of themselves above and beyond the call of duty is now the norm. As your world continues and civilization adapts to a new normal, this is to continue and make your people better for it.

Remember this and act upon it. Do not intend to find the normal of the past for it is not to be found. Go forward in a better mindset and intention—together you will reveal what your people and your world can show at their best. Trust in this and trust in yourselves.

Pax, what would our future, in a best-case scenario, look like if we grew from this experience?

The world-as-you-know-it is a better place for a time of self-examination. A time of impatience with what does not serve the highest and best interests of all results in less value to be placed on economics and more on personal wellness. This does not mean that financial wellness is unimportant, it means the pivot in importance has taken place with love and health and family values taking priority. A time to reflect on what has been and what should be once again.

There is a resetting of the economy on the world stage, a shift in the way of managing business and personal: a new balance not so much created, yet as resulting from a need to adjust methods. Business becomes a different place in the minds of your people. It becomes more of sharing and concern for others and less the cutthroat methods used when it is "all for one," instead of "one for all" mentality.

The balance of family and work changed due to the work from home requirement for many—it remains in place and a daily commute to office and home is no longer the way as home is office for many. A trickle-down effect is resumption of family time spent together, meals taken together.

In many cases, home-schooling remaining the practice in place of brick and mortar buildings housing children as a glorified day-care allowing parents to follow their business pursuits as priority-one. Closeness and togetherness and caring retake their high-priority place in your society, much like a repeat of the past when the world was a simpler place and families cared for families and families cared also for neighbors. This had become a memory and now sees resurgence among your people. It is a good thing.

Again, *if* we learned from this, ideally, what would our food procurement be like in a post-coronavirus world?

As history begins to repeat itself in many aspects of life, eating locally and growing some plants in home containers becomes more of a value to families. It becomes also a teaching tool for children who know so little about their food sources other than the grocery store as supplier. That diminishment in personal knowledge led to the demise of interest in home gardening or community gardens—these see a resurgence where dirt is available and interest is keen. Also a source of air purification: what can be grown organically feeds the soil, cleans the air, and contributes to family health. These practices are embraced by your children and recognition of their value serves to inspire young gardeners and a shift in values follows—another good thing.

This *is* a silver lining. What else, Pax?

We wish to discuss the friendly people who make up the small towns and villages of your world and what they have that your large cities and people do not, and how the learning of their attributes will improve the lifestyles of city people. And this is the truth that will not want to be heard by many but it is the case.

When your world was new, there were a few people and few animals and great resources. Gradually this balance has shifted until it is in the reverse now in your time. Why do you think this has happened? Is it lack of concern, unawareness, inattention or greed? We are here to say the reasons are many and varied and some or all may apply to most of your peoples. Whatever the reasons identified, they can be changed.

Speaking of the trend now towards globalization without care for the old village-to-raise-a-child idea, we believe this is contributing to the downfall of your people today. For you to consider this small town atmosphere of old and investigate how life was, how people cared for people, this is the key to your present as well as your future.

Please know that the time of jet-setting and isolation has its place, but in the overall scheme of things the flourishing of the human race was built on friendship, trust and hard work. Now it is time to return to these virtues. Life moves slowly in some time zones and quickly in others, and the difference is a person's expectation.

We are here to say that there is the need for all people to stand up for your environment and for themselves as guarantors of the repair to the planet.

All people are charged with the responsibility of bringing order out of chaos: the practice of wise stewardship of the land in their daily actions so that their behaviors become that which others emulate. Take the cloth bag to the grocery store, recycle, compost, and plant and harvest family gardens. This is a family project and brings the lesson right to home, as well as wonderful and fresh produce—vegetables from the home garden, grown and attended by the children and parents, what a lasting lesson to teach. It is the highest and best good of the land and the family unit together.

This is the way of the future, as it was the way of the past, we now ask you to bring it forward: back to the future again.

Moving ahead in time we see this as a practice in cities and rural areas equally: rooftop gardens and window box gardens, planter boxes, all individualized and able to support whatever it is that the family or individual chooses to produce. Small amounts of rotating crops, numerous little boxes will grow salads and vegetables usable all year. It is the way again to preserve or freeze or learn how to treat organic goods so they will have another incarnation in frozen or dried form. Much to learn and it all helps the planet.

We are pleased to see this is an interest of the many at this time, and more focus is to be placed on supporting those to make goods and services available to ensure city folk learn what they need in order to be successful.

The bounty that is harvested from individual gardens also instills gratitude to Mother Earth for allowing the nutrients in the soil to cherish and support the growth of good organic products. Pride and happiness in a job well done also attends this activity and it is wonderful to see the whole big picture come together on the days of harvest.

Go forward in this knowledge and this activity.

What a wonderful instruction. Thank you.

If we could have a glimmer of advancements to come, how will we manage a pandemic virus in the far-off future?

The ability to manage wellness comes from a combination of intention and a high degree of evolution in physical make-up. Your human beings have far to go on this path, but do not despair, when the *intention* is placed on the consideration of making it reality that humans become immune, change happens.

The trajectory for this is many generations in future.

Yet, it's possible that we can simply set an intention to be immune from a virus and therefore be immune?

It is the way, yes, and it is evident in the use of a placebo.

When a pill is taken that is believed to have the power to cure, it is often revealed that the cure was experienced. That the pill was a placebo did not result in the cure—it was the belief of the person taking the pill that they would be cured that created the cure.

It is the power of the mind, which controls the physical body at work in this situation. Therefore, to set the intention to not succumb to an illness or not contract a virus, for example, will be the overarching mechanism of healing and prevention both. The power of the mind's intention is not to be denied. The body hears everything the mind says, and when the mind says all will be well, the body sets about ensuring it is so.

What else do we need to know about our immune systems?

It is your knowledge now that pollution of natural resources is a source of dis-ease on your Planet Earth—this is a fact that has long been understood while not acted upon sufficiently.

Pollution is breaking down our immune systems?

It (your immune systems) has become a mess given the world pollution: your people are not equipped to remain strong and healthy and resistant to bugs and disease of all kinds. Your depletion of immunity and resistance is continuing to escalate and it is a sad state of affairs.

How can we begin to strengthen our immunity?

We take you back to the beginning, which is the need to clean your Earth of pollutants so your air and water and soils may once again be relied on to supply clean and pure and healthy living resources.

So much to consider on your Earth and so few considering.

Now that your world is in crisis with "COVID-19" infecting the weak and the strong, it has become necessary to re-evaluate what the world has become. As your skies clear and your waters clear, your breathing air is refreshed and the sounds of silence fill the space usually occupied by the din of civilization, a rejuvenation of your Mother Earth is underway.

It is hoped that wisdom prevails and, when your doors reopen to life outside, protection of these resources will be top of mind. This is to be a new normal like reverting to times of the past where localized living and love thy neighbor were the themes of the day, to bring these forward to present day provides an adoption of the purity of the past which can reinvent the present. This will be a pleasant and desirable outcome going forward.

It is the time, now, to know that malevolent energy is in place on your Earth plane. It is the covering of time and place now by leaders of nations that have not the best interests of the people or humanity at large, in their intentions. There is to be a reckoning for them, and at this time it is wise to be forewarned and forearmed by your own ability to protect your health and wealth and happiness.

Your population follows blindly the leaders who have only personal interest in the future, particularly in wealth and power for themselves—shameful we say. And sad, it is that your leaders are rarely challenged in this behavior. What is to become of your civilization if this continues? Look to history for that answer.

It is beyond time now for your people to rise up and look around themselves, see where they have given away their power to others who abuse the gift by acting in selfish and self-aggrandizing ways—this is intolerable, we say, and your people need to reconsider their actions and become their own leaders. Your world needs honesty and inclusivity and will benefit from the people beginning to speak their truth to power. It is the way to turn the ship to a positive course. Trust in this.

PART FOUR
THE BUTTERFLY MESSAGE

All leads back to our empowerment; you're making this clear.

Your people are at a disadvantage when they give their lives over to others for management. This includes medical and legal and government direction in their lives. This is not bad in itself, but your people are to know it is for each of them to have the final say, make the final decision regarding their wellness, lifestyle, profession— all aspects of life are a choice and the ultimate choice should be theirs.

Be aware that your microcosm of life is controlled by you, so do not fear but be aware of what goes on around the world and the potential for impact. Remain peaceful and live life in this peace, and love.

At this time we wish to impart the principle of trust-in-self, and belief, and moving ahead in your own time and with your own intentions in place.

There is no *one* fix for this pandemic and state of dis-ease on a personal, familial or global level. It is for each individual to do what they feel is best for themselves and then trust in their decision.

New beginnings are now the need. Move ahead in trust that you will create a new world, one changed by lessons learned during this virus time about the value of family and wellness and love and caring and appreciation for all people. A great equalizer, this virus, and the good that can come from these lessons will serve you well. Remember them.

Pax, on this topic, at this time, for this writing, may you please share a final message of comfort to all of the people around the world who are suffering physically, emotionally, financially, and from loss and stress?

Yours is the ability to make a difference in your life and the lives of many. To think locally as well as globally, to act locally and plan globally for a resumption of common sense and wisdom to prevail among your people and your governments—this is a plan, which involves personal power being understood and appreciated.

Your ability now to move ahead in wellness exists. It is for each person to know they may lead in their journey to physical and emotional wellness. There is an upside to this presently experienced upside-down world, and it comes as you open to the possibility of change being made by each person.

We are here to say the Butterfly Message should be listened to and copied by peoples of your Earth.

What is the Butterfly Message?

Consider the beautiful butterfly and its' origins. From the worm to the beauty, how is it that the transformation is effected? How simple does it appear? How truly convoluted and complicated it is.

In the infancy of the butterfly it is a worm, simple and unassuming; much like your world in the overall scheme of things.

What happens then? It goes to sleep for awhile and emerges as a delicate beauty. Your Earth did that eons ago and became a delicate beauty.

Then your people went to sleep and forgot about the care and feeding and the delicate part of the equation—now where are you in the cycle?

Your Earth is transforming back into a worm with your people ready to go into their cocoons to escape the dead air and water. Until such time as these are cleaned up, your people, and your

Earth, cannot emerge again into a state of delicate beauty.

What will it take for you all to understand
and act upon this? Time becomes short—take
the steps necessary to awaken to the need.

Spend time sending healing energy to your
family, your friends, your neighbors and your
country as well as the entire planet.

Visualize this healing energy settling over
these people and areas, and speak your intention that wellness may return. This is yours to
offer the world and yours to manage. Personal
power leads to personal wellness and you have
the capacity for both. Love prevails and love
overcomes all.

**Thank you, Pax, for your message to humanity. That
was beautiful. And still, don't want to let you go. I don't
want to leave it here. I feel overwhelmed. Our people
will feel overwhelmed. We need more words of hope
and encouragement from you.**

Our final words are hopeful and realistic. There
is no silver lining today, there could be tomor-
row (if you create it), but it is to each person to
create their own. There is no wholesale government rescue coming. This is a lesson: this may
be the lesson of this time.

Each of you is to contribute your best in all
ways you can.

Each person has the power and we ask them to know this, do not diminish it, believe in self and your new life in the new normal of your Likely Future. It will be right for you.

It is our wish for the people of your Planet Earth that it is understood this current-day virus is decimating the population. Looking back into your history will be found others considered natural disasters, plagues and pestilence that did the same. Always the people overcame these blocks to the happiness and progress of their time. Always the people found new strengths within themselves, and always the people designed new ways of living and going forward. Always the people became stronger for it and because of it, and always the people prevailed.

This is a historical view of your people and their strengths. Your world has changed but your people remain strong and dedicated to the preservation of their families and their communities. It is this core-strength that shows itself now in your population where the strong become stronger and the weakest among you see this and take the lesson for themselves.

Your people are not victims, your people are warriors and it is at this time that their true spirit shines brightly for all to see, to emulate, to be proud of and to transform their own selves into the peaceful warrior spirit needed to rise above this adversity. It will be.

Your people are imbued with the knowledge of how to move forward and to each we say, trust in yourselves and go in peace and love.

—Pax

MESSAGE FROM PAX IN CONTINUATION OF OUR JOURNEY

We are here to say it is our pleasure to continue the work with Carole Serene and Penelope and it is our gift to them and theirs to me. We have anguished over the plight of Planet Earth and your climate crisis. We have ideas and direction that could be of assistance in turning this around to healing. It has been our gift to speak through your people.

It is the case that we have much to contribute going forward and wish to speak as soon as possible. It interests us that this project spreads to those with wide influence, thereby elevating our message to a higher speed of distribution.

We continue with works beyond this book and know Earth people are trying for planetary repair—we believe and contribute.

Trust in this and go in peace and love.

—Pax

ABOUT THE AUTHOR AND CHANNELER

Penelope Jean Hayes is a new consciousness author, television contributor, and speaker. She has appeared on-camera hundreds of times as an expert guest on programs including *Dr. Phil*, *ABC News*, and internationally. She is the author of the book *The Magic of Viral Energy: An Ancient Key to Happiness, Empowerment, and Purpose*, and the series *Do Unto Earth: It's Not Too Late*. Penelope lives in Naples, Florida, with her husband, Burt.

In 2019, Penelope was invited by Pax to author his messages (as channeled by Carole Serene). As explained by Pax, Penelope's soul journey spans numerous lifetimes with a longstanding mission for Earth wellness.

Carole Serene is a former nurse and longtime student of metaphysics. Carole has been channeling Spirit since the early 1990s, when she was chosen by Pax and given the title "Spirit Messenger." Writing and providing in-person as well as remote sessions for clients around

the globe continues, and Carole refers to her gift of channeling as "the greatest blessing in my life."

The work of this trio continues—as Pax says, "a good
team we three."

www.PaxWisdom.com

Made in the USA
Columbia, SC
10 July 2020